hope dealer

First published in Great Britain in 2021 by Turqoise Quill Press
an imprint of Not From This Planet

Copyright © 2021 by Catriona Messenger
Cover Design by madappledesigns
Formatting by madappledesigns

ISBN: 978-1-912257-61-4

First Edition

hope dealer

Poetry by
Catriona Messenger

Turquoise
Quill
Press

They came

They came and gifted me with treasure
Erikka and Ingrid

Where I grew up

Cumbria, the place I grew up
Where silence became my very best friend
Empty but full
Brimming with the feeling of 'alive'
I knew my fields, my woods and my river
And they knew me
My tree
Crawling carefully across your root
Curved outwards
Sturdy
I sit relaxing into you gently holding me
My river below
Freely flowing under my feet
Twittering birds and talking leaves – I tingle
Held – oh the love my tree has for me
And I for my tree
I am sure the world is beautiful
My tree and my river whisper that it is
Hmmm, I agree
And so does the fish, as he breaks our silent chatter
With his flippity flop – catching a fly
I don't quite know what heaven is
I am only 7
Still, I feel sure where I am is it!
'Yes, I agree', says my tree

Everything matters

Everything matters
Nothing is wasted
All moments
Noticed or unnoticed
There for the taking
Constant communication
If we willingly take part
Slow down and take note
Quietly hear
Observantly see
Openly feel
Courageously acknowledge
Our full self
The piles of experience
Depths of emotion
There for the taking

A conversation

It's a conversation I think I didn't want
The challenges of belief come grappling around me
Stories now running wild inside me
They're enjoying a fantastical party
Rampaging in circles, gathering friends
They shout and clamour about having life
Smothering mine, but I stand apart
Their rambunctious activity grabs me
My attention - I'm watching and seeing
Above the confusion and the churning
Now they wish they hadn't shouted so loud
Their behaviour reminded me, I can choose
Join the party or not and the party dies down
I chose not and the stories all leave
Carrying disappointment and empty bottles
I feel them disappearing
Peace returns – wow – I choose

Derwentwater, Friar's Crag

Sitting above you, my feet on rock
My bottom, on a thoughtfully placed bench
I ask you…
And you wash over me
The sound of your cells colliding
It is the buzz of connection
The voice of the world
All its cells moving together
Including mine
You flow over and through me
Joining us, we are one
All at once – bonded together
Free of separation
I am one with the world
As are you
This tingling dance of life
Moves me
Swiftly and easily
Circulating, fluidly
Through my flesh

And hard bones!
How I delight in flowing like you do
Ever changing – as you are
With the wind
The rain, the Cumbrian skies
Different, but in truth the same
With every visit
We share contemplation
You show me with mastery
The way life is when true essence prevails
That strengthens my ground
I am rich, abundant...
I tear myself away
Letting others sit with your wisdom
My heart is open
I ask...
'Stay with me'
I know I'll be complacent
Allowing my true essence to fade
I will need your teaching again

I feel like a child

I feel like a child
In a world full of 'grown ups'!
My heart wants childlike innocence
Wants to see a world that means nothing
Open to exploration from emptiness
I feel ill-equipped and unprepared
Like I know nothing and don't understand
Everything the 'grown ups' speak of
Makes no sense, sounding strangely odd
I don't want this confusion, take it
I want to give it back and start again
With nothing
Turn me over and empty me out
I want to see again
A world that is empty - fullness
An empty heart that is full
Full of Light

Always Loved

A new story will unfold, what is past is gone
blame or judgement can't rewrite a wrong
Look to me, your Spirit inside
ask for my Help and we'll turn this tide
There's help in you, singing in your heart
I'll show you in truth, you play a beautiful part
Help you to heal, let go of what's gone
God's Divine Love, writes in you, a new Song

Egoic storm

The egoic storms navigated by travellers
Stories that blow and gust through mind
Rattling doors, throwing dust on windows
Stripping leaves from limbs, bending signs
Gathering litter in circles, debris
Leaving stories behind to be cleared
Work to be done, restoring and renewing
Whether a rose bush that now needs pruning
Supported, or devastated lives that need rebuilding
There is opportunity for beauty to be born
From clearing the stories of the egoic storm

Dance

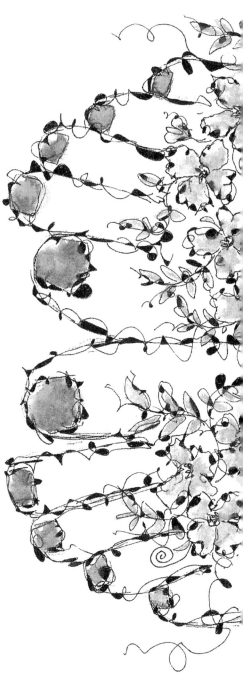

Dance Yes Dance
So I do as my heart breaks
A bit
And tears flow
As I Dance, Yes I Dance

I want you to shine
Let go of life's stories
I want you
Shining through them
Dance Yes Dance

Brave

I want to be that brave
To let my wild wilderness out
Whole worlds that live inside me
Where All is beautiful
All has purpose and interlocks
With golden thread and energetic suns
A head filled with freakish dreams
And dynamic wandering across
Non-sensical lands
A heart bursting with Love
For possibilities and Miracles
A soul swimming to the depths
Of green and blue and red and black
Always finding treasures
I want to be that brave
To turn this world inside out

Where wonder and awe have no limits
They find opportunity everywhere
To show up and up and up
Where my footsteps appear in front of me
And there are wings on my back
Hands holding me and carrying me
Gentle is a given
And courage too
Because fear is wrapped in Love
With animals carrying scrolls of
Letters and life-giving messages
The trees they draw in heaven
And breathe it into my lungs
Flowers grow across my eyes
I have cherished friends in every heart
I want to be that brave

After a light filled day

After a light filled day
Why does the dark come
So the light can come again
Would we pray for the light
If the dark did not come
The dark is a gift
It has messages
It is filled with asking
Abundant with prayer
Leading us into expansion
Towards another, somewhat brighter
Light filled day
And the dance continues

Already written

In my mist and fog
That rolls over mountains
Settling into deep valleys
Impossible to see?
I'm asking for help
I need a guide to navigate
Paths with no view
Across haggard ground
Well-trodden, new ones waiting
To be walked, laid out
Uncovered, new views
Stretching out to different lands
I need a guide and you come
It's already written, echoing
From mountain rock, singing
Into the valley's below
The way is written, the path
Under your feet, is the way
You can't be lost, I found you
With no wrong signs to follow
Your only task is walking
Towards Love, planting
Your feet with Love
Instead of fear
Here to walk with Love

Expectations

Expectations are pain
Comparisons burn
Suffering webbed into
Ideas and concepts
When experience
And expectations
Don't match
We suffer with wrongness
We label as victim
We tell stories of loss
Betrayal is ours
Regrets are ripe
We suffer

What if life
Has a different face
What if our concepts and ideas
Are flawed
Limited
Fencing in Happiness
Barricading Joy
What if I choose
Unlimited
Moving the barricades
Embracing the face of Love
Choosing Happiness
What if?

Gold

I hear you gently whispering me in
So sweet are these drops of Gold
Drip drip drip, they steadily fill my heart
Mixing with my imaginings and blood

Shhh be quiet, I want to listen
I'm in Love with my drops of Gold
Drip drip drip, they gently speak a rhythm
Creating with my heart and mind

Hmmm I see you glistening in edges
Everything laced with drops of Gold
Drip drip drip, an orchestra is playing
Liquefying life in molten treasure

Ahhh delight, delight together in gifts
So rich we are in drops of Gold
Drip drip drip, abundant Love always given
We are the heavens in drops of Gold

And we grow

The garden of my soul needs water, replenishing, cleansing
I need harsh heavy rains that drench my soul
with angry storms that frighten me and wake me up!
Days of mizzle and drizzle, low clouds tumbling over my
sorrow
and the sun's rainbows soaking my joy
I need food, nourishment for strong roots and beating heart
I need dark death and decay to know and enrich my soul
and the light bursting new life to heal it
I need birth – struggle, striving, held with courage, reaching
for the air
The light, the life beyond the bosom of the
earth holding me safe
I need the wind that batters me, rips at my
delicate naive shoots
and leaves me scarred, but strengthens my
core
I need gentility of tender attention at my
own hands and of others
sorting through the beds of my life, finding my
way to bloom
I may be heavy come autumn, releasing the
lessons of my soul
falling back to the earth, to be held
In the cold emptiness of winter, I will sleep,
for this is my heart's desire

Re-birthed when spring comes, I will grow
again
with the vigour of knowledge and the
strength of Love, I ask for what I need
And summer is mine, I bask in the sincerity
of the beauty of Life
the sun's delicious caress, warming my heart
and acknowledging my soul

Loss and Gain

Sometimes 'the world' feels so beautiful
I might burst, Love fills me up so full
It feels too big for me to hold
Love might explode me

My seams are splitting, I'm coming undone
I'll be obliterated into empty space
This day it came, I'm bursting with Love
And my seams did split

Love boomed through me
And expanded out, I felt the explosion
Emotion poured out, pain having to leave
How can I be so filled with Love?

I perceive the greatest loss, yet
In the jolt, of the Love, breaking out
The energetic ripples, of all that is
Charged across the unknown

The answer came, filling empty space
In flowed, 'because loss is not the Truth'
'Gain is the Truth', Love is something else!
Real Love, not how we think it is?

An Ode to my Children

Oh, my delightful babes
Your revels are at their beginning
Made from the fabric of the earth
Be spirited – love is your way
Wear this worldly illusion loosely
Grace is substantial, the rest will fade
Leave forgiveness in your wake
You are such stuff as love is made of
May your lives be rounded with peace

Thanks, Will

Forget what we've been told

Buying into beautiful
Has been today's pursuit
Myriad opportunities delivered
To paint with dynamic colours
And reach into an endless depth
Of miraculous gifts - given
Feeling the fullness of Joy
So bountiful and blessed
But then I hear it
It creeps in, seeps in
That voice – but without a sound
That feeling – but not in fervour
That image – but nothing sincere
-It's not right to feel Joyful
-When you have lost
-Something must be wrong!
-Don't deny your pain
-Are you bad
-Did you not Love your beautiful one!
Yes, I did, with all my heart
With all the life I perceive to have

And infinitely more than that
And with all her heart, her Joy
I know these deadly utterings
Are not my truth
They gather and pull at me
I know it's attacking myself
Fear based thoughts with personal design
Ego stitching its egoic dream world
Dream catchers weigh heavy
Above our heads
Saturated day and night
Feathers and beads – poisoned
This is not Love
As the attack ensues
This pulling feeling
An agreement to be torn
Love awaits my recognition
Awaits my willingness
Ready for my asking
Graciously answering my call
There is a haul of pain inside

Remembering what I've been told
I can meet my pain with Love
On this park bench
In companion's gentle conversation
The middle of a song
The eyes of another
Witnessing a moment of kindness
I'll meet my pain with Love
What's pulling at me
This mixing pot of delusion
A potion laced with distress
Can I stop listening
To what I'm being sold?
Forget my egoic lies, born of egoic world
Walk the road of ready and willing
Can I listen with Love instead?

Forever
broken heart

A forever broken heart
has fractures through which
abundant Light shines

Dearest One

Follow the callings of your heart
They will be louder than the shouts of fear
When I ask for Life to come through you
And you believe you have nothing to offer
Your heart will tell you, My Love
Tell you, I do not agree
Your ego lies, I speak only Truth
Yes, you want to follow that truth
And the lies will speak of pain, but
My Love will always save you
Love will always hold you
Two worlds, one insane
The other is Glorious
Heaven on Earth
Life's beautiful Truth
Yes, it's always been in your dreams
It's always been in my heart
Waiting to be found
Journeying into oneness
Towards Life's Truth
Love has carried you
Always

A moment

The glory of a moment
That astounded me
The beauty of that script
That put Life in me
Gifting healing
The only purpose there is
To be washed with forgiveness
To witness harbingers of truth
A glorious moment walking
The leading edge of Love

Bowscale tarn

She lay still and gracious
Surrounded by company
Bold and mighty friends
Her hidden depths held
In their tremendous strength
She knows her own beauty
Sharing it with all whose eyes
Land on her, pausing and
Acknowledging her
Some think she is cold, unmoving
Others see peaceful tranquillity
Whether seen or not
There is gentle oneness
With those around her

Follow

Follow me down these imprinted pathways
Communication that takes us somewhere
What speaks out for healing
Healed in me, expanded in you
Riches that flow from the troublesome
Healing rendered from the painful
Change unfolding from unruly emotion
Gifts declared from vulnerable truths
Giants embrace the unwanted
Hearts swell and burst
In acknowledgement and a loving welcome
Tears fill rivers that wash and nourish
All as beautiful, all as glorious
As celebration, delight and awe
All held in peace and gently expanded with joy
Everything without exception
Is Abundant with Love
Just follow

Heaven on Earth

It's not supposed to be like this
The little girl said to the snail
It's not supposed to be like this
You know that don't you
She shouted to the whale

The grasshoppers hummed their gracious song
As the little girl walked by
She marvelled at the clouds
She raised her arms, swooped down the hillside
Connected with the birds in the sky

Upon a wave of daises sewn through the grass
She lay down for a natter
Look how intricate your beauty is
You know how special you are
And a Bee buzzed in to join the chatter

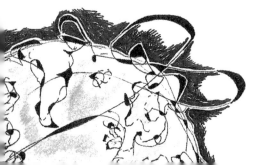

It's not supposed to be a fight
It's not supposed to be right and wrong
The grass, the trees, the sea, the fish
They don't fight to be right
They sing a harmonious song

The river gave company to the little girl
As she walked the last path home
'River' she proclaimed 'they've all forgotten'
She stopped and looked at the rivers flow
They've forgotten who they are and I wish they could know

River you would show them if they looked
You always comfort me
You make me tingle with Your Love
When I feel your flow, I see you
When I see you, you show me, me

Existential Crisis

Taken to the edge of oblivion
Everything doth fall
And an emptiness is left
Which frightens at first
Terrified even?
Perhaps we close our eyes
Not willing to let go
Of the falling away
Who am I, might emanate from us
Not knowing anything, anymore
May be our current rhythm
Left afloat on a vast ocean
But I am afloat
The ocean is carrying me
I'm asked to look at my dress
On it, beautiful flowers bloom
They spread to my raft and grow
Lush grass now covering it too
And outwards, across the ocean
Creating a meadow for my feet
An invitation to walk
I might not know where
But I have an invitation
And I want to accept it

Giving thanks

Giving thanks
to all this life
collections of pain
gatherings of grief
heavy freight
lining up to be healed
brought to us by comrades
angels disguised as devils
giving thanks to collaboration
our willingness to take part
to do this for love
sorrow and joy
fear and love
mourning and celebration
harrow and beauty
giving thanks to embracing it all
fully human
full of potential for healing
gracious respect to us all
courageous human being
journeying the mountains
and ravines back to love
giving thanks to you.

Come through Me

What can be done with this
My experiences
Seen through this
Known with this
That has never been known before?
What can break through
Shine in from this
Tell me, show me
No, just bring it
Deliver it through me
I'm Yours to shine Light
Hold me in Your Hands
Director of Light
Let Your fingerprints, be Mine
Let me touch this World
With my True Identity
Let me be my unknown

Blessed

Show me the garden of your soul
The honest beauty of who you are
As I watch you grow this is my wish
Show me the garden of your soul

Ask and it is Given

Love, Healer and Guide
Are unravelling me
All that is not true inside
The more unravelling there is
The more space there is
For spirit to fill me
And fill me spirit does
Heal me spirit does
Change me spirit does
Love me spirit does
I feel the flow of alive
Travelling around
My emptier flesh and bones
Generating new Life

Pulsating within
Something other than old dreams
Decreasing deaths hold on me
What is it to be truly alive in truth,
I admit I do not know
But if it be even a fraction
More beautiful
than the Love infiltrating me now
My mind continues to be blown
Into dust
And an illusional world
Can shrink smaller
Than the tiniest fragment

I am, I am

I am a universe
Filled with black emptiness
Which in truth is Light

What can't be seen, still exists
What isn't seen, is most Real

I have stars and moons
Planets of life
I am All of Light
My truth is buried
By limited eyes

What can't be seen, still exists
What isn't seen, is most Real

Always

For every stab of pain
A zillion kisses of life
For every fear filled story
A zillion calls to truth
For every broken heart
A zillion bursts of light
                    Always calling you

For every lonely road
A zillion footsteps with yours
For every heavy burden
A zillion feathered wings
For every dead-end path
A zillion open doors
                    Always answering your call

For every perceived failure
A zillion expanded worlds
For every moment in grief
A zillion ribbons of Love
For every forgotten certainty
A zillion beautiful pearls
                    I am your strength
                              You are my light
                                        Always

Being

Being 'alive' is a story
Many soulful threads
Woven, elaborate tapestry
The stories we choose
Ones we give attention to
Give energy and life to
It's then the world we see
We can choose the stories
We weave and tend
The world we see

Gardening

I'm coming in from outside
Hanging up my coat
My work is done
I swept the leaf litter
Laid it for compost
I dug the weeds to clear space
For treasured blooms
I pruned branches to strive
For a fruitful harvest
Mowed the lawn to keep it
Thick with growth and healthy
I'm tired, so worn out, aching
I forgot the gardener, that works
In my garden, that work is done
The gardener came ahead of me
Oversaw it all, every detail
Created to perfection
In the world of forgetting
I see mess and chaos of jobs
Undone and unsolved problems
Work that I must take on
In the world of remembering
I am released into freedom
From gardening, I just enjoy
The Perfect scenery

Life is my Bible

Life is my Bible
In constant communication with me
And I with life
The query
Am I paying attention?
Sometimes I may slumber

Let go

Let go
Losing sight of separation
Declaring hearts written
With the same script
We really are the same
Here to heal, teachers of Love
Restoring truth, seekers
One moment with one other
Just one moment, with one
Is enough
One empty moment, carrying
Nothing
Will change the world
I want to carry nothing
I want to teach and learn
Real Love

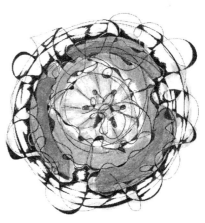

god
holds
all

God holds all
What is written is there
In writing
On angel's wings
We were delivered
To do this
Forgiveness
Life to be healed
Not undone
And we are held
So gently held
Playing out these stories
Compelled to act
Upholding our agreement
To bring it all home
To gather in
And stitch the wound

We cannot stray
From laid down path
But we can paint glory
Colouring the steps with Love
Agreeing to be medicine
And in hearts that agreed
To be transplanted
Is given every gift
That can be given
Graciously walking us through
Honouring our service
Supported in every stride
Warriors of Love
Givers of Healing
Bringers of truth
And so, it is

It's all in you

The answer
To every question
The solution
To every challenge
The acceptance
For every healing
The wisdom
For all growth
The stillness
To bring peace
The forgiveness
Deleting grievances
The truth
To bring joy
The Light
Underneath it all
The Real Love
Who you really are
It's all in you
You are the Light
Of the world
When you see it
In you
You'll see it in all

Life speaks to us

Life speaks to us
Are we listening
Life sings to us
Can we hear
Life shares secrets
And gives the pieces
To build a world

Everyday

Let a little bit out everyday
Sitting on the edge of the bed
Leaning into the sink
Toothbrush in mouth
Chewing a bite of sandwich
Let tears fall for a moment
Everyday

How brilliant
our stories are

How brilliant our stories are
Worthy of space on any
bookstore shelf

Not understood Love

I want to write Love songs
No fickles of love
The kinda Love that built a world
And many, many worlds
Love that writes itself into lives
And creates abundant experiences
Handwritten adventures
Mysteries between pages
Spilling blood
Healing wounds
To create more Love
Pressing itself into itself
Holding us in myriad meanings
Contradictions and chaos
Truly, truly beautiful
The richly unknowable
Not understood Love songs

How is it possible

How is it possible
To feel so broken
So utterly broken
And so Loved
So utterly Loved
All at once?

Ego

Doing your number
Playing your game
You hide and puppeteer
I forget I'm looking for you
And give in to you pulling the strings

But now I see you, I've been asking
To understand and spirit answers
Light has lifted and your cover is blown
The dark corners are lit, nowhere to sculk
You're plain in sight playing the strings

I see you with your list of tricks
Reading them out and acting out
Gosh your skills are poor in shining light
All your weaknesses, there to be seen
Powerless, gosh, small and powerless

I asked for help and spirit shone
I rubbed my eyes in the light of Love
Is this the truth, you're nothing
But a trickster, selling hidden lies
In dark corners, I buy them no more!

Return to sender, now
You have nothing I want
We'll walk our differing ways
I will keep asking and rubbing my eyes
In spirits light, in Love

I am everything

The bit of me that doesn't know
How do I get up in the morning and feel
any happiness at all
And the bit of me that knows
I feel happiness because it's not an
external thing
It's an internal decision
The part of me that wants her back and
aches every second
And the part of me that knows we signed
up for this
Knowing it has glorious Divine purpose
We are courageous!
That part of me that deeply has struggle
And that part of me that always has trust
Everything is there
I am whole when I acknowledge it all
I can feed these parts of me as I wish
Create from that which is being fed
It's all okay, Perfect even

Good and Bad

Good and Bad, right and wrong
All stories, concocted and shared
Flowing in and out of these pages
Searching for a story with a gift
Something that feels momentarily
'Better', and the search continues
It all expands and one day we'll meet

In Rumi's field

It's all for forgiveness

It's all for forgiveness
Seeing the truth
All a beautiful purpose
To Earth us with Love
To heal us with Heaven
Walking the deathly valley
Combining the fragmented
Experiencing this prism
Riding this rainbow homeward bound
Returning to one, to Real
To Love unknown

Healing

Your healing is as important to me as my own
You are me and I am you, we are one
The world keeps this a secret, but
When I look at you, I see myself
This is the hidden truth
If I see the need for healing in you
There is healing needed in me too
Ask for healing, it is for all
It is for loving this world as one
Anywhere I see brokenness
It resides somewhere in me
If I ask for healing for myself
And find willingness to receive
Heaven on earth can be believed

Love's Adventure

I'm doing it anyway
regardless of the stories
I tell myself
in other people's faces
or expressions in words
Sometimes my story is
to listen to an outside self
But now my story is
listening to an inside self
And so it goes this epic tale
so beautifully scripted
what is written will be
Flowing pages upon pages
blown up in cosmic winds
landing on earthly plains, rolling
across this written landscape
Building hearts from stories
expanding Love's adventure

Many rules?
Are all our fears and pains
Born
From many rules
Love resides in only
One
The rules that speak
Of truth
Of heart
Of oneness
Compassion
Love
Flowing through all
Dancing with life
There are no exceptions
In truth
All is held in Love

Many rules?

Exceptions
Many rules
Rules that
Halt the dance
Stab our hearts
Break us down
Box us in
Chain us up
Create chaos
Havoc
Suffering
Where are we?
In Love
Or in exceptions
One rule
Or
Many rules?

Light and Dark

As Light and Dark exist in separation
The world exists in separation
As we hold Light and Dark apart
We see right and wrong
Us and them
Me and the other
The world pushed through mesh
Divided into opinions
This or that
Opposing sides
One way or this way
Choose!
What is beyond choice
More than choosing Light or Dark
Beyond separation

The ideas of right and wrong
Rumi's field – The Truth
Light and Dark are the same
One thing
Beyond dualism
There is only one
All that is – is the same
Not split, not categorised
No war of accepted and not acceptable
No torn up, diluted, weakened
Broken, diminished, destructed
What does the Truth look like?
All is one, only oneness
Fullness, wholeness, true acceptance
Light and Dark are the same
Are one thing

Sight

Sight is short
On their own would our eyes be unaware?
That what is seen has any meaning at all
Meaning is added
A deluge from other sources within us
And yes, they are windows
Our aperture to the world
The world's aperture to who we truly are
Can you afford to look past your own filters to see me
What do the eyes see without filters
Without the deluge of meaning
Carried on pathways from the past
What would our eyes see if we were born again?
Looking through a window with emptiness
So clear, would the reflection be perfect
And that is all that would be seen – perfection?

Hope

Reaching to understand it all
I see in me, reaching for Hope
But Hope belongs to me
It is a given
With Faith and Love
It is our complete
Our whole
It is who we really are
If I already have Hope
Then I can stop looking
It's in my heart, my hands
My feet, on my road
I can wear it as shoes
And drink it like water
It flows always with abundance
I can stop looking for Hope
Outside of myself
Where it seems hidden
In confusion
It rests easy in emptiness
In three, inside
Inside is everything
There is nothing to hold
It forever flows
Hope

A condition?

If your compassion has conditions
It isn't really compassion
If the statement we're all one
In this together, has exceptions
It can't be your truth
If Loving kindness has to be deserved
That isn't Love at all
If acceptance is only given
When your standards are met
You will be forever tormented
If generosity is guarded
No generosity exists
If beauty requires judgment
Beautiful is not what you are seeing
If your heart has restrictions
You're not fully alive

Blue

I feel you in the edges of things forgotten
Parts of me I don't allow
Beautiful me that dulls that light
Your fingers running over those blue notes
Freeing my beautiful hidden self
Surfacing blue waves touched by sun
Catching my light, giving it breath
Crashing over the sandy edge of me
Onto the new shores of my home

A Love letter from God

You - My physical manifestation of My Love
That's the secret that I whisper in your ear
The truth buried in your heart
The reality beyond the smoke and mirrors
I Love you - I say
Precious child, I created
From the glory of this Earth
You came into being
I wanted you and truly always do
Your heart may be hampered
Broken even, by the lies of a fallen world
I know who you really are
You are Mine
Trust Me - your heart is bringing you back to your Creator
I am your Father, your Mother
The One who nurtured you into life
The One who nurtures you still
From the inside out
Can you feel Me inside you?
Loving you back to Me
Cherishing every cell of your body
Every thought in your mind
Every word from your mouth

Loving the beautiful perfume of the richness of you
The richness of the gifts you have given this world
On your journey back to Me
Can you feel the depths of My Love?
It's beyond anything you can imagine right now!
Can you feel My tears?
My tears of sadness for your suffering
My tears of joy for your healing
They fall upon you and wash you with My Love
You know it, My Love, deep inside
That Golden thread I attached to you
Keeping you with Me
No matter what
Come My child, be heartened
You are My warrior of Love
You are Love
My Love
Always

To transcend it all

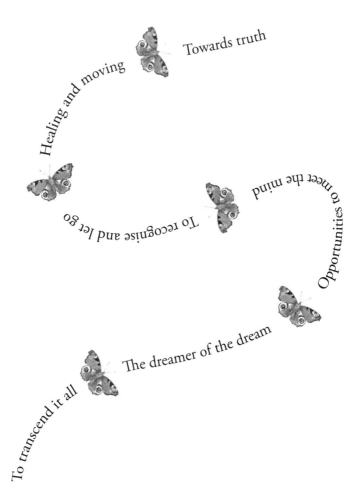

Towards truth

Healing and moving

To recognise and let go

To meet the mind

Opportunities

The dreamer of the dream

To transcend it all

We do not know

We do not know
The beauty of everything
The greatness
Without exception
God's Love expanded
From what seems to be
The tiniest current
What looks like a trickle
In truth all beautiful
We do not know
The greatness
Without exception
God's Love expanded
From the seemingly
Dynamic and glorious
What looks like a waterfall
In truth all beautiful
The quiet, the gregarious
The trivial, the substantial
In truth all the same
We do not know
Yet we can glimpse
If we choose to look
And truly see
The beauty of everything
God's Love expanded

Little things

The worth of little things
What is it that attracts us
when in our life we see benefit
in the little things?
I love the phrase
 'it's simple to be happy, but it's not easy to be simple.'
The little things keep us simple
the more there is, the more complex is, is!
Complex is full, it might be described as rich
but it's not simple. Complex is busy
heavy, weighty, it's multi-layered
and complicated! Complex needs understanding
investigation and study
it needs cleaning up, maintenance
and constant attention
Does that sound like a lot of work?
Little things are simple, simple is easy
light, effortless, singular
and empty. There is nothing to understand
or work out. Simple can move freely
and come and go with ease.
Ahh, the little things give us relief
connecting us to simplicity
which is a key to happiness
Little things really are the big things

Heaven I'm home

Heaven I'm home
  You never really left
Yes, I've been dreaming
Now I'm awake
  It's good to see you

If you know who you are

I'm telling you that Life
wants us to know who we really are
Don't point to the heavens
the gurus, the angels and saints
Listen to them and find them
inside yourself
That's the truth of where
Truth is, in you, in me
We are the heavens
the gurus, the angels and saints
and when you truly know
Who you truly are
Heaven opens up inside you
Love can flow, the Real stuff
like you've never felt before
The unconditional stuff
looking like compassion
opening forgiveness
and your worldly stories
will start to fall away
Things you've held on to
where anger is cooked up
and black and white thinking

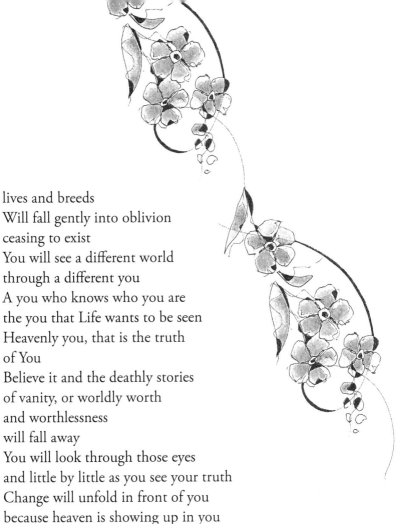

lives and breeds
Will fall gently into oblivion
ceasing to exist
You will see a different world
through a different you
A you who knows who you are
the you that Life wants to be seen
Heavenly you, that is the truth
of You
Believe it and the deathly stories
of vanity, or worldly worth
and worthlessness
will fall away
You will look through those eyes
and little by little as you see your truth
Change will unfold in front of you
because heaven is showing up in you

Keep Hope

Your feet will keep stepping
Towards me, you are in Love
I am in Love, relentlessly
I pursue you as you pursue me
Whether you remember or not
I have you, my Love, my true Love
You won't fail to find home
It's written into your heartbeats
Inked under your skin
Recorded into a rhythm
That plays out in you
Right now you might not see it
Not hear it, struggle to touch it
Keep Hope
Your feet are stepping into me
In every moment Real Love
Is yours, whether you remember
Or not, you will. The writing
Speaks of remembering
Your foundations, your Reality
In me, you are mine
And I am yours, take me
You are bursting with Real Love
Ask and I'll show you it's true
So true, relentlessly I Love you

Way pavers

Beyond perceptions of right and wrong
I see way pavers, and
they don't have to stand out to be counted
No need to be recorded in history
to be a Gift to the world

Inside

I don't want to talk about who did what
And who said what
And what is wrong and right
Can it not be seen
This behaviour is still a fight
Still a battle, still a war
Still a room filled with closed doors

I don't want to talk about blame
Who's a victim and who is not
But always see this opportunity
To work through my own lot
To ask why do I think this
Why do I feel this way
What are my fellow humans showing me
I want to ask, I want to pray

What is this dysfunction blocking me
From seeing the more beautiful world
What are my feelings gifting me
Are my thoughts in Love or in fear
How can I see this differently
How can I remember to choose
In sleepy reaction, we all lose
Wake up and feel the discord
I really want what's true
Wake up and ask to be brave
To see something new

My tolerance for fear is waning
It's hitting an all-time low
How much can I forget myself
Refusing to listen and grow
It seems we all self-persecute
Painful self-sabotage
Everything is an opportunity
To explore what we really are
My world, my reflection
My perfect agreement to be told
What is asking to be healed
What inside can I unfold

Oh Love, drench me now and forever
Keep prodding me out of sleep
When I hear you loud and clear
But refuse to let your voice speak
Hold me tight in your Love
Show me my fear thoughts beneath
One step at a time, hold me steady
For Love I am here
To let go, I wish to be ready

Life holds me wherever I go

I say as I sink deeply within
What am I looking for? Nothing
It is a letting go of all that appears to be
Movement away from the dream
Into expansion
Beyond constructs
Into the open mind

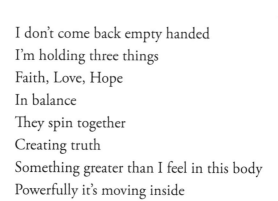

I don't come back empty handed
I'm holding three things
Faith, Love, Hope
In balance
They spin together
Creating truth
Something greater than I feel in this body
Powerfully it's moving inside

Deeply beyond this perception
Holding me differently
Turning clearer pages
Unwrapping layers
Opening this horizon
Knocking down some edges
Penetrating the dream
Changing a reality
Molten Life creating new land

Living

Living expressions
Called life
Crazy, beautiful
Chaotic
Running through
A twinkle here
Sparking there
Pulsing, Oscillating
From nothing
We recognise
Or understand
How beautiful
To be an expression
Left in wonder
Without knowledge
Of the empty void
That gives life
Chaotic, living
Expression
Of not-known

Here and Now

Can we meet where we are?
Then there is Hope
That truth will be known
Time is fuel for judgement
Beyond ideas, concepts
Right and wrong
There is here and now
Let's not introduce
Let us bestow
Only this moment
Every moment
Now
It is an honour
To meet you
To be met by you
Here
What a beautiful truth
To ask for nothing
Let go of fear
Hold steadfast in faith
Create Hope
Engender Love
Here and Now

It does not look like Love

Were you taken from us?
Why?
Random accident?
Cruel unjust act?
With no sense or reason!
A kind, loving, gentle soul
Why should she go?
A world so rich in pain, fear, abuse
And a gentle, loving soul
Who poured love into the world
Has been snatched away!?
I am human, these are my questions
Something pours from my achingly
Wounded heart
Is there Love in this brokenness
And suffering?
The loss of our gentle soul
Still a child
Illusions they hurt like hell!
Where is the Light?
The Love?
The Light of Love that breaks illusions
Breaking us

Opening us up
Showing us a path beyond
What appears to meet blinded eyes
Was it always to be this way?
Agreed by all involved
To endure grief
Broken is open
The sorrow that we are all so closed
So tightly bound by fear
By lies
The illusions of this world
That tragedy is necessary
To break our hearts
Open us to the truth
Allow Light in from spirit
Opened by loss
The bravery of souls to endure loss
For an eternal plan
Feeling like huge sacrifice
A journey to Love
Love is not just the Light
It is the Dark that drives us
In our search for Light

I love you, precious girl
I love you too, Mum

Mysteries

Her own mysteries held deep inside
Protected by a misty veil
Over her watery depths
She holds a tall, sturdy light for others
Are they lost?
Outstretched is her arm
She is battered by waves from the world
Longing for the strength of her own Love
Her rocky foundations could erode
Into her ocean, her light could drown
Her outstretched arm does lift
Her, looking into the depths
Does hold her, as she sees herself
Reflected in the ocean
She is the light of the world
Her foundations resolute
Made by Love
When truth is seen
The mist rolls out and there it is
All her mysteries are her Miracles

Red

There it is, a deep red dangerous pool
Inside me, red with anger
Filled with all my pain
Human life pushed away, scared to look
What is there to be afraid of?
Only fear itself, but fear is not the truth
I call to Love and listen to answers
I walk with the trees and ask to be healed
As I dive into the deep red pool
Life comes alive in me
This pool is filled with courage
Determination, within
It is a pool of Hope
I am drenched in Hope

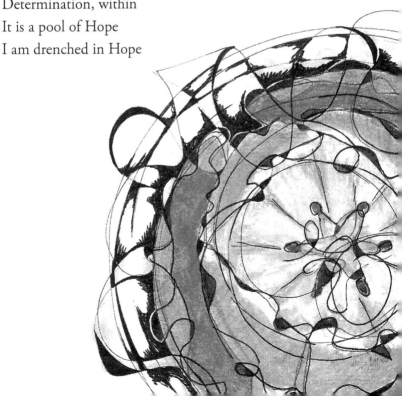

Say hello and goodbye

Say hello and goodbye to stories

Invite 'Nothing' in to stay

Yellow

The mower came and cut you down
You responded with growth
Movement through cycles
You will grow again
Your life is a circle
Changing with the environment
Being a dandelion
The best dandelion you can be
In the environment you find yourself
A happy yellow that calls out, bees come
Calling out gets you picked, but still you grow
It's windy today, perfect for spreading your seeds
Far and wide, bringing joy to lovers of yellow
And displeasure to haters of weeds
Who decided to label you this way
That's not how you see yourself for sure
You are an example in this world
Playing your vigorously, yellow, delightful part

Let me be filled

Your mighty truth
Fills me
Let it fill me
Let it spill from me
Your mighty dreams
Expand me
Let me be expanded
May I be mighty
Your infinite generosity
Astounds me
Let me be astounded
May I express this generously
Your beauty draws in
My every breath
May your beauty always be
My air
Your Love washes me
The essence of all
Flowing like water
Always finding a way
May I be submerged
In your everflowing Love

Silver

The silver lit night sky, casts a slit of itself across my wall
A heavy heart rests in my chest as I lay on my bed
As sleep befalls my wondering mind and wandering soul
I'm asking...
What do you want from me, this strange girl
Who stays quiet, so quiet with your Love?
Guarding it fiercely, not that anyone would know
Asking for your help in a world that makes no sense
And perfect sense all at once
Asking, asking, asking
What do you want from this girl?

New Year's Resolution

Love, please help me be yours
In a world that mostly teaches us to close up
To protect ourselves, to live in fear.
Can I spend my time being courageous enough
Vulnerable enough, to open up
Opening my heart to undo what has been learnt
And listen to Love instead
Can I choose being awake rather than
The slumber of allowing my ego to run my life
Love – please help me be yours.
I wish that I can recognise Love in everyone
Who they really are, not just when it is easy
But when it's hard
When my ego-based beliefs are in the way – wake up!
Would the world be the more beautiful place my heart knows
Do our hearts open
When the Love we truly are
Is given recognition from another
The precious gift of unconditional Love
Can I wake up and see who I really am – see my heart
Can I choose, rather than running the old over again
Can I choose to listen to Love instead
A gift to myself that can then be given
Love – please help me be yours.

Touched

I adore your music
I delight in the truth
That runs through me
As I listen to you
As I notice
That which stirs inside
Deeply somewhere
Unknown, I connect
With Divine Truth
Through your Love
Of who you are
Subscribing to self-
Remembering
The energy of this
Glides over my edges
Effortlessly reviving life
Breaking in
To the beautiful
Waiting to be known

What more should we ask

What more should we ask in this
Universe so vast
Nothing more than to know
to feel and to see
The Loving Light of Our Truth
is all we need be

Perhaps

Perhaps we cannot alter
That which is sewn into the fabric of life
Our offering is
We can choose how we respond

A glitch

What is this dream
Walking stairs, I've walked
A thousand times
Acknowledging a notion
I've never trodden them before
Déjà vu's opposite?
How did this moment arrive
What came afore
What could be thereafter
Held in stasis
A sudden feeling toward
Nothing, no man's land
Of how did I arrive here
What is this hypnogogic lapse
Moments ago, so real
The world is odd
In between pages
Without numbers
That truly have no order
Maybe space was needed
As something
Was being newly written

What I give to you, you find inside

What I give to you

And what's given to me I'll find that too

Only Love in this dream

We are all in energetic agreements
Mining for beautiful truth
For Love
Every connection
Every tender touch and violent act
The guy we walk past and judge
The person in the news that touches our home
The cat that claims us, the dog that waits all day for us
The stubbed toes releasing anger and tears
The emotions that stay with us some years
The stories we believe and the tales we deem tall
The times our eyes rise and times our hearts fall
The sun that shines persistently, rain that fills rivers with floods
The beliefs of good and bad, shouldn't and should
Agreed with Love for Love
Touching your hand, a moment of truth can be seen
No strangers here, only Love in this dream

Whispers

What do you whisper in my ear
endless Love poems
that I, only sometimes hear
What truth do you lay down upon my heart
that a protective shell keeps Love apart
Asking is always a path with clues
asking for Love
to find a way through

I reach for those stars

I reach for those stars
And touch them with ease
I have strength
I have courage
My heart loves
I am free
I walk this life
With purpose
With peace
I am the earth

I am the heavens
I'm here to learn
I'm here to teach
Life flows through me
As I dance along
I am powerful
I am gentle
My heart sings my song
I can see truth
I can hear it
Feel it in all of me
All I came here to be
I shine my light
Always safe in Love
Love holds me true
I see your light
I see your Love
I see truth in you

One

Judgements deposit in banks of separation
Opinions holding us in separate heads
I don't want to make more fear filled deposits
Or think separate thoughts in a cut off head
I'm asking to let go of these ego ideas
Fear based thoughts and concepts
This is my asking, to leave the separate world
To walk into a more Loving world instead
Where I meet myself round every corner
I meet myself in every face and voice
In every view, big and small, far and near
There I am, this is me, there is only One
Let me forget what fear sounds like
Let me hear only the true calls of Love
Where we are all the same thing
Experiencing All possible things

Remembering

The things that we do
Born from the story book of our life
Teaching us we are far, far, less
Than our glorious truth
We are the Light, powerful
Wholly compassionate beings
The world taught us to forget
But memories are given
Our truth is a given
The memories of this beautiful truth
Are to be shared, to remind us all

Lift

A tide moves over my head
A great wave of bird
The roaring break of wings
Pull my energy, lifting me up
Bringing me to the present
Back where I belong
Where they never left
Together, I join their flight
Lifted in connection to Life.

Not-Love

You live in me and speak
You speak to me of not-love
Not-love wrapped up, separated
Into boxes of belief
You come up seemingly without invitation
What does not-love want from me
I want Love, I come into your room for healing
Presents for presence to heal
Turned over into treasures of truth
There is love in pain and suffering
Turned over to presence
Turned into truth
Heal ourselves heal the world
Not-Love, is Love
Waiting to be recognised

Old tattered jumper

Old tattered jumper
It's hard to let you go
Who am I without you
We're tired and torn
With holes from life
Holes that let in the cold
And threads that catch
You want to unravel
Bare, threadless
What then?
I'm busy blaming the world
For wearing you thin
Trying not to see your holes
Wanting so to be whole
And carrying on.
Unravel you will
Seen or not
You are mine
If I'm willing to own you
Love and treasure you
Could I accept your unravelling
And knit you anew?

One mind

One mind
Access to it all
Where do you find yourself
In any moment
You can choose
It's all available
It's all one mind
Find yourself in fear
Find yourself in Love
Where can you move yourself?
What appears to be happening?
It's always opportunity
To see what's happening inside you
Where in mind you are
Where do you want to find yourself
In mind

Silence

Your silence fills me up and overflows me
Full and richly woven with Love
The gentle tapestry that holds life together
Love refracted plays through our grooves
Delightfully we are etched in wonder and awe
I feel the awe of you in the depths of silence
Falling into you is Love so true, so alive
Faithfully, knowing, your orchestration, I am safe

Recycling

Recycling
Nothing is wasted
Unloved or unused
All the 'old' bits
Become the 'new' bits
Imagine a cocoon
Wrapped round a caterpillar
What wonders are inside
How life metaphorizes
Recycling legs
Into wings
Even the casing
That drops to the ground
Becomes soil
For fertile hearts

Yeah

Yeah, a story that feels better is the way to feel better,
but even a better story can be challenged.
No story, is where peace is, where *nothing* can't be challenged.

The Wedding of Life and Love

Marry me with Life and Love

Do you agree

To Live?

I Do

Do you agree

To Hold and Cherish Love no matter what?

I Do

Do you agree

To see Truth beyond what appears to be, choosing
Forgiveness instead?

I Do

Will you Grow

Nurturing Empathy and Compassion?

I Will

Will you Trust

In Love when it appears the world is broken?

I Will

Will you keep listening

For Love when Life breaks you and makes you Bleed?

I Will

Will you Remember

You are Love, as is everyone and everything else?

I Will

Do you promise

To wield your sword Gently in search for Heaven on Earth?

I Do

Know this;

Love promises to Hold you no matter what

Love has given you a Golden thread

This can never be broken, however far you stray

Love will always see you with Forgiveness

That never changes

Love promises to wake you up each day

Reminding you who you really are, when you lose your way

Love will only ask of you

That which you have the Strength to endure

Love will never leave you, Love is yours Forever

Love, you desire this Union?

I Do

I now proclaim that you are Love and Life as One

Go forth and Live, with Life, with Love, Now and Forever

Amen

Now Celebrate!

You are a swatch of my Love

You are a swatch of my Love
I cut you from my cloth
I imagined you with perfection
And perfection is what I got

When you are ragged and crumpled
And feeling out of shape
So sure, you are not good enough
You know, this is not a mistake

Doubt, shame, unworthiness
Even fear, Love unfolds within
How can you create true beauty?
If you don't experience Sin

My heart desires Heaven on earth
And beyond this veil it is known
Brave hearted one you've stepped outside
And mighty, oh you grow!

With broken hearts battles are won
With loss, blood and tears
You came here to do this
I'm championing you; can you hear?

Stand up and demand that I tell you
How faithful you have been
I'll sing my Love into your heart
Listen; for you are always seen

I Love you now and always
And as your dynamic work comes home
You'll rest upon an infinite joy
At how the world does grow

Yes

Yes, I will
I will sit still
To be moved and moulded
I open up and invite you in
To do your work
I will give up my opinions
Let go of my beliefs
To hear your truth instead
I'll stop second guessing
Attacking and regretting
No more planning
Or fear-filled plotting
Grasping and netting
Have it all
Use it all
I'm ready for you
It's time for you
I give it all
To you…

Pieces

We all have a jigsaw puzzle
Placing in the pieces
Creating pictures as we build
We don't make the same image
Our pieces are different shapes
The shape of you
Is the shape of your pieces
The shape of your world
Myriad images being placed
Into a perfectly designed puzzle

Love
be me

Love be me
And flow
Through me
Glorious
Love be
Our truth
Heal
And shine
Let us say
Yes, to you
Heavenly
And be
All I see
Generosity
Gentle
Strength
Blooming
Growing
Heady heights
Of Love

What if?

What if there is more to
this than meets the eye?

What if this could
be seen differently?

What if this is showing me
something I need to know?

What if I was to follow
this emotion and thought,
would I find wisdom?

What if I let go of these
beliefs and concepts, what
treasure might I find?

What if there is
always Love?

Traveller

My body drops into exhaustion
I am ready to allow stillness to come
Allow myself to be called forth by the light
That keeps travellers safe, heals them
Guides them, all in creative hands
In the peace of these truths
I will sit quietly and wait
Infinite patience of Love

The gift of tears

Always I thank you
For the gift of tears
A severing of ties
Opening of boxes
Releasing the old
With thanks
With humble knowledge
It's time to move
Reflecting a want
For healing
In glistening droplets
Rolling down
Warm cheeks
Sometimes wiped away
Sometimes allowed
To fall beyond
I might have to decide to breathe
I might not notice
If I am or not
But there is movement
In tears
Beautiful release
Releasing healing
In me
And you
Thank you for
The gift of tears

Nothing to do

What is this ease
What is this peace
The movement of life
It flows continuously
Unaided, completely natural
Life will flow, you will grow
There is nothing to do
Just be and watch and see
Life flows and life grows
With or without you
So just be

The caterpillar does nothing
But exist, watch the metamorphosis
The tree does nothing
But exist, yet mighty it may grow
The sea does nothing
But exist, sustaining life itself
The earth does nothing
But exist, everything in collaboration

Nothing to do
Just be

Stillness

Gusting and blowing
About my ears
Your breath sounds
It plays your song
Through the trees
Wind mills whirling
A chattering voice
When you blow
Stillness is alive
Moving
Shuffling, bustling
Making space
For something else
My Healing
Finding me in stillness

What is this Joy

What is this Joy
To be God's paintbrush
Thick with colours
Painted purely
With Love

What is this sorrow
To forget who I am
To be bristling alone
On a messy canvas
Confused

What is this Joy
To remember and let go
To be held by a creative Hand
To be moved
With Love

What is this sorrow
To feel separation
To be the fake artist
Brushstrokes of fiction
Confused

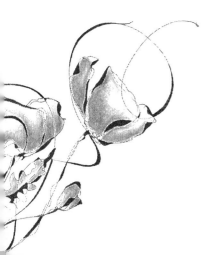

What is this Love
To return Home
Following Heavenly inspiration
Painting Hearts and Healing
With Love

Light in me

I'm aware of her all the time
her presence feels to be indescribable
For some experiences words cannot be found
words that might give the truth of this
do they exist. Words, I ponder images
as a picture pieces together in my head
like colourful snowflakes caught in a whirl of wind
Gathering an image of this beautiful girl
in burgundy flower traced chiffon
A joyous dance in the wind
these snowflakes merge together
forming an image of her, the sun now shines
across her beautiful smiling face
She is a light in me
I'm aware of her all the time

We

We're all hearing something different
We're all seeing something different
Feeling something different
In seemingly the same things

The happy dream

Can we live the happy dream
The dream that is the real dream
Led by Spirit, in joyful mind
Expansive lightness, soaking hearts
Drawing Heavenly thoughts together
Peaceful walks across steady ground
Harmonious notes dipped with Love
Gentle breezes moving rhythms
Delightfully changing seasons
Abundance is carried in boats
Down zestful rivers of compassion
To the open Ocean, saline Glory
Guided, Healed, Held in Creative Hands

'The Mystery Begins When'

The mystery begins when we open a door
A door that's never been opened before
It doesn't need a key, just a willingness to look
Behind a door, that's never been opened before

With trepidation, a little ajar, a chink of light stuns my sight
Overwhelmed, I turn away, maybe not today
There's enough to do, life's hard enough
To be doing something unknown and new

This is familiar, with a false sense of control
A mystery unfolding is no good, I need to know
Show me the highlights, behind the door
Then maybe I'll open it a little bit more

Give me some guarantees,
My ideas of what life should be giving me
I'll welcome a mystery, that's not a mystery at all
My knees hurt too much, I can't bear a fall

Living in a world that's not truly mine
I'll numb out my feelings with busyness and no time
Not looking at the door, pretending it's not there
Making do with satisfactory, I kid myself I don't care

But I do, I do care

The door will continue to make itself known
The faintest of remembered tunes it will gently hum
When 'normal' becomes intolerable, the handle I grab
Fling the door open, shielding myself from something bad

Light washes over me and the mystery begins
A new story is beginning, put the old one in the bin!

Stories

Stories look for validation, Truth does not

Travelling Light

I'm packing my bags to it all
No, I'm not taking bags
I'm leaving it all on the platform
No thanks, no thanks
Send it for recycling
Return it to the sender
I don't want it
It never belonged to me anyway
I gave in and I carried it
And now I travel light to be healed
This return journey
Outward bound – hurray
One direction – the kingdom
Stamp my ticket
I kept it in my pocket
Ready for the yielding
The 'I can't carry this anymore'
The train approaches
I wave goodbye
There are others on board
Travelling light, they wave me in
The journey back home begins

Tangled

Tangled lines
We gently pulsate within
You are never the same version I see
Always changing as, I am
All possibilities running parallel
We dance along seemingly
Back and forth
In and out
Of who we are now
And now
All happening simultaneously
Landing focus here
There
This
That
All running along tangled lines
All possible perceptions
Seemingly perceived
Gloriously aware
Or unaware
Flowing towards truth
The only thing that is real

We are the flower

We are the flower that opens in the sun,
Closing up when dusk has come

The promise

That we agreed
You'd wake me up and hold her tight
The three of Angels spoken in Love
Reminding us to look beyond
To know how beautiful truth is
Even in pain
Everything is ok
We promised to do this
With Love

The ego is a vampire

The ego is a vampire
It disintegrates in the light
It's dances in the dark
It moves, it shakes
It hedges its bets
To bring home winnings
Quenching a thirst
To survive, to thrive
Sneakily
Demanding attention
Without waking you up
In sink the teeth and claws
Draining you into submission
Walking death

You are the light
Egos disintegration
Wake up, dance
Move and shake
Hedge your bets
Bring home the winnings
Quench Loves thirst
For truth, for healing
Openly
Demanding attention
Waking up a sleepy world
Fulfilling Loves calling
Walking Life

You are tired

You are tired
And pained
Heavy
Don't be burdened
By a load
My hands carry
My feet guide
Let this be so
You are Loved

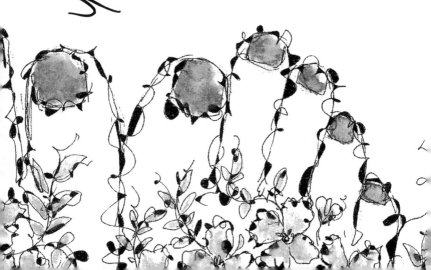

Veiled Crowns

We're all adorned in crowns
It is our rightful dress
I crown you, there is the truth
Love, who you are beyond
Delusions of underdressing
Relinquished thrones
Standing empty
As guilt keeps us small
And burdened and riddled
With lies and dis-ease
A death in silken deceit
We veiled our crowns
But there is hope in a prayer
To unveil the world
In asking to see your crown
This uncovers mine to you
We are Kings born of Kingdom
Unveil yourself
Let us Live, Crowned

Without stories

Without stories, there is only Love

Only Love

I knew it
The truth
There
From the beginning
Always
Though there is no end
It's all
Perfect
Beautiful
There is nothing
Wrong
It does not exist
Not that way
We see
Even wrong
Is right
Right is all

There is
Only Love
Is real
Not looking
Like Love
Not sounding
Like Love
Not feeling
Like Love
Look
Listen
Feel
With your heart
Instead
There is
Truly
Only Love

Walk

Walk with me I say
As I pass between trees
Walk with me I say
To the biting autumn breeze
Hold me I ask
Hearing my feet in the leaves
Cherish me I say
As sun melts the nights freeze

I am all that I have
For the truth to be known
If I'm all that I have
Then Love must be shown

Take me I'm yours
I demand of the sky
Take me I'm yours
Birds soak my ears as you fly
You're beautiful I claim
On all that I am
You are beautiful I bless
Life filling this land

Oh, radiant Love
I command you flow
Like rivers of life only you know
Compelled to journey to sea to home

With the wind that blows grief away
And rain that drowns yesterdays

These Loving pastures will grow
From seeds so graciously sown
Oh, beautiful Love
I command that you grow

I am all that I have
For the truth to be known
If I'm all that I have
Only Love I will show

Walk with me freedom
Silent mountain peaks
Take heart with me
Fear in unknown streets
I ask to be carried
Walking miles of snow
I ask you for gifts
Wings to soar valleys below

I am all that I have
For this truth to be known
If I'm all that I have
Let Love be shown

We are a channel

For Love in this world
For Healing towards heaven
Through us, human 'Life'
Healing wounds of separation
The journey back to Love
Back to One
Who we are, not separate
Not lost, not abandoned
Only Love, always Loved
Embrace this experience
You are a channel for healing
Mending the threads
Bringing together the pieces
Lining it all with Golden Light
Flowing through hearts
In minds, we heal together
Channels for the writing
Of Heaven's great works
In Love's hands
Through us

We know not
what they
are doing

We know not what they are doing

but it is perfectly unfolding towards Love

Our Bliss

Our Bliss
Arriving with nothingness
Wrapped in a blanket of sleepy forgetfulness
Born from emptiness
Left at the edge of the river
Which flows abundantly with fear
Its waters rise and fall
Rise and fall
Helpless it drags us in
Our harrow;
We only have this blanket – sleepy forgetfulness
The grabbing fear collides with innocence
Carving out unwanted tracks
Stealing truth from under us
Severed roots
We flow along to unknown lands

Infiltrated – distorted – broken
This river is rich with grit, stones and rocks
Distressed eyes, scarred skin, battered hearts
How long before the blanket is torn and ragged
Bitten, ripped and blighted
Falling away
Tired and torn, it's fading
We slept!
We slept so we could wake up
Wake up – it's time
Remember emptiness
Our homeland
Deep roots and clear water
Balanced eyes, healed skin, revived heart
Self-remembering
Our bliss

Why did I come

Why did I come, why did I agree
To endure this story that displeases me
You came, you shone, you left us here
Left us here to drown in tears?
Am I cross, yes with this world I am
Pain and heartache of this eternal plan
All for change, change is the cause
Brushing up against our bravery is scorned applause
This all sits tight across my chest
This heavy feeling, the need to have some rest
Don't fall into a human sorry sack
Where thinking of only me becomes self-attack
For We not Me, this is the broken human role
What can I do with my determined soul?

What is dead, with death is now alive
Let my bleeding heart pump out my pain, but strive
Bleed out into the world this truth from my veins
Love is forever, it never dies or wanes
Come to life world, death has brought to sight
The depth of Love and its true Might
Never ending, unlimited, boundlessly strewn
Across the universe, because of death there is bloom
I may look handicapped through a slumbered mind
In truth I bare wounds from which Love can shine
Yes, I came here and this loss is agony for me
But for We I accept it was meant to be
For change, for Love, boundlessly strewn
Infinite, unconditional, Love coming into bloom

Slip inwards often

Buffeted by the broken minded world
Illusionary winds lift our edges into waves
This surface becomes chaotic and stressed
White water crashing over us
It's only a fraction into the depths
Of who we really are
Our water goes on forever
Deeper than we know
Reaching under the breaking waves
Find stillness – holding us
The gentle infinite soul we are
What is this life experience?
That has us grabbing for the oars
In a bruised and battered boat
Sometimes almost crushed

By our surface waters reaction to the weather
Let go…
Fall…
Into ourselves
The depths of who we really are
Slip inwards – often
Where our water is clear
Is calm
Peaceful, serene
And steady
No boat, no oars – held deeply
We are absolute
In our nourishing liquidity within

When baby cries

The deepest part of my being is stirred
Distressed is your call in me
As I drown in the watery grasp of others
Their words of peril, their judgements
Their theories of your well-being
They burn and blister my heart
Your pain of confusion is loud
It's a match to my own
I want to hold you
Comfort you, whenever you ask
Whenever you want me
And I want you
Every moment of mine is yours
I declare it so
My heart devoted to give to you
Unconditionally, freely
But there are many traps
Snares of fear, judgement, blame
I fall to my knees and bleed
As your cries come from my soul
This is not how it's meant to be
My Love for you wants to be free

Orchestration, synchronicity

Records of musical notes
Elaborately synced
Joyous collaboration
So happily, I welcome
Each perfect coordination
The melody flows
Even when my ears are closed
Perfect lyrics have been etched
In time, without time
The libretto flows
Even when my eyes are closed
But how precious indeed
When I hear, when I see
The glorious inscription
Of orchestration
Of synchronicity

The world feels lighter

And when the world feels lighter
looks brighter and deeply beautiful
On a day that you discovered the beauty
of you, another acceptance into yourself
This Light-filled worldly expression
with your name and face
One of billions of faces of unfolding Love
Honoured as you look in the mirror
and see a tremendous part in a story

When you take the shackles off
whatever they might be made of
It's something heavy that held you apart
kept you away from your Divine Truth
That was perfect and now you know it
the perfection of your expression
in its entirety, no exceptions
You truly are the light of the world

It's an honour to be asked, to hold
these precious tasks given to us
To bring the Light, expand the Light
I bow my head, that I
have been entrusted
with such fine treasure
Royal broken hearts
Golden grief and heavy jewelled
It's all Love crowned on our heads

What if All is intentional?

To discover what it is to be lost
to be confused, seeing a world
that creates asking to know
Purpose built illusions
to experience All, All can be
What if we're ready to see beauty
where it was not seen before
Ready to let go of hopelessness
regaining trust in what's Real
Remember All is perfect
remembering Love exists
where fear appears to be

That which seems abhorrent
is courageous under-cover work indeed
That loss does not exist
and Gain is a truth
And broken hearts are true
and beautiful
Love speaking to us, through us
are we starting to listen
Hear our loneliness that speaks
this precious song of Love
leading our journey on
to new worlds

All Holy

Share humble respect to the Holy
That they bless you with Holy encounter
See the Light that shines from grief
And the Love that flows in sickness
Bow to those, trodden down
They are Mighty indeed
Let yourself be raised up by them
Those that are seemingly low
Have Heaven in their palms
Have Miracles in their eyes
Waiting to be shared with a world
In which their Truth can be seen

Perfect as the imperfect

How imperfect I am
Contemplating perfection
How perfect I am
Contemplating imperfection
Many layers of me
To touch, to feel, to see
Things remembered
And things forgotten
Depths of knowing
And vague unknown
Taste and smells
Triggering and delighting
Surging emotions
And fleeting wins
Skin and bones
Blood and cells
Movement and colour
Spinning together
On a spinning world
I am an expression
Of dancing towards heaven
I am beautiful
I am miraculous
I am perfectly imperfect

What do we get

What do we get if we bring Light and Dark back together?

Love instead

There are no winners only losers
In blame, anger and grievance
The world will not thank you
For adding more pain
More dark skies and raging water
More devilish winds and parched desert
Fires and wars, chaos wins
In grievances, anger and blame
When life serves up the unwanted
Walk with a different world
Find something other to believe in
Listen to songs and reach
For different messages
Look at faces and search
For kindness and compassion
Listen to the backdrop of life
And hear an orchestra playing
Try
The world does not need more pain
Ask to find Love instead

Time

When time stops
A falling away
Emptying
Letting go
Times crock of
Concepts
Evaporates
Edges disappear
Everything
For a moment
Can be known
A vast emptiness
A different love
That holds nothing
Complete
Silence
Peace filled
Nothingness
Love filled
Emptiness
When the earth
Is still
When real touches us
Truth knocks it all
Out of us
Then time stops

Stories

Thieves of peace
Trying to hold the unholdable
Opinions, judgments – a story
Exceptions, expectations – a story
All things that are not things at all
It's all one shining light
Everything attached, no ends
No beginnings, no gaps and edges
The stories create seeming separation
Just stories causing ideas and concepts
Dividing up that which in truth
Has no division, one expression
Of all the Unimaginable
Let go of stories
Find peace

I imagine

Our glorious plan
That all hurts like hell
I imagine
The mountains forming
As continents collide
The earth forced upwards
Creating tremendous peaks
So steadily, rumbling, raising up
Pressure causing change
Life does this to us
Life collides with us
Causing pressure
Creating change
Beyond the initial crumbling
And distortion
The ensuing destruction of collision
Comes an uprising
Vertical lift
Towards the heavens
Glory in this growth
That hurts

Capital letter Love

I was asked
What do you love?
I'm profoundly in love
With Love
Not falling in love with another
Falling in Love with myself
This kinda Love, is deserving
Of a capital letter
This kinda Love
Resides inside all
In everything
Inner Love, that reaches out
To the brink of the universe
Expanding always
Present always
Am I in touch with this?
My infinite, endless Love

Where expectations are lost
Conditions make no sense
Challenges are opportunities
Good and bad dissolve
Trust is inherent
Edges become blurry
As all becomes one
Faith is a given
In capital letter Love
For myself
Heaven on Earth is felt
And building it begins
From the inside out
This capital letter Love
For Sure
It's the greatest Love

I want to talk about Love

She waxed lyrical in her mind
Of the energy that moves mountains
Inside her
She felt it flow
Whooshing through her corridors
Flinging open her windows
And doors
Bubbling, leaping, skipping
Light as Angels feathers
Drifting in Love
She waxed lyrical without any words
An old story playing in its grooves
An undercurrent of belief:
Who wants to talk about Love
When what seems wanted is fear
This gobbled her words
Before her lips could grace them
Crushed, buried
And this was the yielding
Falling into hopelessness
No hope?

Two worlds, Love and fear
Agitated her core between them
Afraid to unravel this fear
Stitched into her seams
She lived her life in fantasy
Lyrical in private
In nature
On paper, filed away
Listening to the hopeless lie
Listening to guilt and shame
But it never left
Love
Always there
Asking to be spoken
Dear one
Gift me lyrical with spoken words
Give your lips to Love
Let me flow freely
I've blown open your windows and doors
Reach out to Hope
Rays will shine
With me
It's a beautiful day

It's not easy being the 'bad guy'

Do you 'hate' me
Do you relish in your
'Someone to blame'
It's all a game!
Cat and mouse
Hide and seek
My role
To hurt, to abuse
Narcissistic madness
Sticking my poisoned
Tongue, into your ears
Stirring up your fears
Do you think I enjoy
Being your 'bad guy'?

Poking and prodding
Ripping and flogging
For you to find your
NO'S and help 'the world' grow
I'm showing you yourself
Your trauma, your beliefs
If you look at them
I can hang up my coat
When you look inside
Give up blame
Heal what fuels your fire
Then I can retire
The 'bad guys' work
Will be done
Healing complete
Love – won!

Nonsense

Nonsense
I ask myself
Why am I doing this?
Am I truly willing to look?
Uncovering my secrets from myself
I may find a book
Of fear-filled nonsense
A ruse
A con
A work of fiction
It makes no sense, fear
Can I bring to light
Fear hiding in the dark
Well disguised
In seemingly 'good stuff'
I may discover quite a haul
Why am I doing this
My mantra for happiness
Unpacking nonsense
On my birthday
At a party
In the car
The restaurant

Social media
The protest
In the gym
My second bar of chocolate
Or bottle of wine
Why am I doing this?
My head will defend
My ego justifies
What does my heart know?
An ache under the weight
Of nonsense
How brave can I be?
Mining guilt
Mining shame
Anger
All rocks of fear
Love will erupt from courage
Diamonds
Truth
The stuff of no question
Unquestionable
Sense

My indigo sea

If I be submerged
In my indigo deep
Diving down
This watery infinite lagoon
Will I be blind
Deaf and helpless
Speechless
Powerless

Swim

Float

Swim

Float

Sink...

What would it be
To sink
Into my deepest archives
Where monsters are alive
Tucked into my crevasses
And caves
Residing in this darkness
Are they embarrassed?

Ugly, shamed
Are there claws
To slice through me
Gnarled hands
To throttle me
For fear of a death
Is there distortion
From heavy words
And spike filled actions
Is that the truth
Of my indigo gloom
If I sink will I be

Consumed
It's another world
Other worlds
All mine
Can I sink
And see what I find
Will I resist with fear
Or hold treasure in mind
Taking Love with me
These monsters
These worlds
Are all mine
An inky indigo canvas
To play with inside
A dark city I created

Cells for the unwanted
What if I give them life
Give beating heart
To my misunderstood
Robes and crowns
To the carcases
Of if only I could
Gifting pearls and diamonds
To regrets and wrongs
Writing poetry and music
Forming a choir of song
With the rabble of me
Who didn't belong
What colour could I bring
In deep indigo worlds
That are of me
I celebrate
This perfect eco-system
My indigo sea

It's all communication

It's *all* communication

About the Author

Writing has always featured in Catriona's life, having been inspired by her poetic grandmother. Not only is it Catriona's favourite way to express herself, it is a safe place to explore inner worlds. Catriona is sure that all the answers to her questions about life, are hiding inside herself. She finds inspiration in the joy of nature and stillness, and in the discomfort of noise and busyness, and has come to realise that it's all communication. She is inspired every day by the stream of thoughts and feelings she experiences, and the awareness of which ones she wants to follow and give life to.

Catriona joined a creative writing group in 2017 called Mungrisdale writers, and other than writing poems for her children when they were young, this was the first time she had shared her poems with others. Writing supported her greatly in her most challenging time, the passing of her 13-year-old daughter, and continues to do so.

Catriona fell in love with ink pens and drawing in her teens and even though over the years she has experimented with many creative ideas, she is always drawn back to this first love. She grew up in Cumbria and continues to live there, happily surrounded by family, friends and pets, hills, trees, rivers and wildlife. A favourite pastime is being out and about with her Border Terrier, Miri.

Also by Turquoise Quill Press

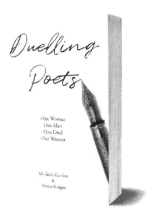

Duelling Poets

One Woman
One Man
One Duel
One Winner

Michelle Gordon
&
Victor Keegan

For 30 days in 2012, Michelle and Victor each wrote a poem a day, taking turns to choose the titles. Michelle is an author, who was in her late 20s at the time, and Victor, a retired journalist in his 70s. Their differing experiences and perspectives created contrasting poems, despite being written about the same theme.In Duelling Poets, we invite you to read the poems and choose your favourites, then at the end, you can see which poet wins the duel for you.

Turquoise Quill Press is an imprint of Not From This Planet.

NotFromThisPlanet.co.uk

Printed in Great Britain
by Amazon

76535742R00106